A Step-by-Step Approach for Success on Written Exams

by Stephen J. Mahoney, Ph. D.

Good Apple

Executive Editor: Jeri Cipriano
Editor: Jeanne Gleason

Good Apple, Inc.
A Division of Frank Schaffer Publications
23740 Hawthorne Blvd.
Torrance, CA 90505-5927

© 1996 Good Apple. All rights reserved. Printed in the United States of America. This publication, or parts thereof, may not be reproduced in any form by photographic, electronic, mechanical, or any other method, for any use including information storage and retrieval, without written permission from the publisher. Student reproducibles excepted.   ISBN: 1-56417-637-1

3 4 5 6 7 8 9 MAL 01 00 99 98

from the **AUTHOR**

As educators we are striving to improve our ability to teach our students to think critically and write logically. At the same time we are also improving the way we assess our students' academic gains. Authentic assessment has become the current model of assessment. It enables educators to evaluate actual student work instead of relying on standardized tests to measure achievement.

In 1993, California implemented the California Learning Assessment System (CLAS), which requires students to respond to a writing prompt. Fourth-, eighth-, and tenth-grade students must now be able to work with other students to gather and use information to write a persuasive essay, stating what they think while trying to persuade the reader that their position is best.

Reason and Write provides students with a simple process to gather and process information critically and then write an essay to logically persuade the reader to agree with their position. Each lesson provides three different writing templates: The beginning template is designed for third- and fourth-grade students, the intermediate template for fourth- through sixth-grade students, and the advanced template for experienced writers in sixth grade and up. (Although the writing activities are too difficult for primary students, these children can do quite well on many of the activities when they are done orally.)

Learning the basic template will provide students with a tool that can be used to write a persuasive, expressive, or evaluative paper for almost any situation. It will also provide structure that will enable eighth- and tenth-grade students to master the more specific genres required on the CLAS: Problem-Solution, Evaluation, Controversial Issues, Speculation About Cause and Effect, and Interpretation.

S.J.M.

Contents

Introduction

Why do you think what you think? This question is the driving force behind this book, the aim of which is to teach students to think about what they think and to develop ideas that support their thoughts, choices, and opinions. Each lesson provides a writing template that enables students to form an opinion or take a position and then support their position in an organized and logical manner. It combines cooperative learning, critical thinking, and the writing process in a way that provides students with the tools necessary to master any assessment program that requires students to write a persuasive or expressive writing sample. *Reason and Write* provides third- through eighth-grade classes with an approach that integrates social studies, science, and language arts with critical thinking activities and writing practice.

Reason and Write **consists of three integrated strands: Teaching the Thinking Taxonomy, Prewriting Activities, and Writing the Essay.**

Teaching the Thinking Taxonomy is a series of activities to introduce, teach, and practice thinking skills from the six levels of the taxonomy: *knowledge, comprehension, application, analysis, synthesis,* and *evaluation*. It uses a collection of common objects that students can touch, see, and feel to teach these skills on a concrete level. Once familiar with these skills and thought processes, students can apply them to more complex problems that require deeper thought and explanation. This critical step develops and establishes the ability to gather and process information to be used later to support their ideas, positions, and opinions.

The Prewriting Activities are planned cooperative-learning activities that use the skills learned in Teaching the Thinking Taxonomy to gather and process information about perplexing questions. Each lesson starts with a question that raises an interesting issue. Cooperative-learning activities then focus on this question. During this part of the lesson, students work together to gather, comprehend, apply, analyze, synthesize, and evaluate information. Some of the Sequential Lessons are subject-specific, and others are more generic in nature. Many of the lessons can be done as oral lessons in primary grades, and most can be done by students in grades three through eight. However, there are some that are more appropriate for intermediate and upper grades.

    Writing the Essay requires students to reduce their ideas and opinions to writing. After completing the Prewriting Activities and student reproducibles in groups, students work independently to form a thesis statement regarding the original lesson question. A simple-to-follow writing template enables students to develop their thesis statements and support their positions in a logical and organized way, using the information gathered and processed during the prewriting phase.

Teaching Thinking Skills

Teaching Thinking Skills

Overview

The activities in this section of *Reason and Write* focus on developing the different thinking skills in the taxonomy. These skills—knowledge, comprehension, application, analysis, synthesis, and evaluation—can be taught in the same way that skills are taught in other subjects, beginning with concrete objects and concepts before moving on to more abstract ideas. For example, a student can learn to compare apples and oranges before learning to compare the ancient Roman and Greek empires. All students can participate no matter what their abilities.

Teaching Thinking Skills
with the
Thinking Box

To make a Thinking Box, collect objects with which students are familiar. School supplies, tools, plastic fruit, and toys are great items to have in your Thinking Box. A well-stocked Thinking Box might include tableware, action figures, plastic animals, string, pliers, chalk, marking pens, and other objects that might show up at school. Add to your box daily; it makes a great place to keep all the things that come to school that aren't supposed to.

The Thinking Box will be used to teach students about knowledge, comprehension, application, analysis, synthesis, and evaluation. Spend 10 to 15 minutes two or three times a week to introduce each level of the taxonomy. Use a chart to record the brainstorming ideas that come from class discussions. Keep these charts posted for comparison as you go through all the levels.

1 Teaching Knowledge

Explain to your students that *knowledge* is knowing facts about something, such as size, color, name, and age. Pull an object out of the Thinking Box and show it to your class. Allow time for students to look at and touch the object. Ask students to think about facts or things they know about the object. After a minute or two, let students share their ideas while you record them on a chart. This is important because students can learn a great deal from the answers of their peers. When students give nonspecific answers, such as "It's little," ask them to clarify their answer by asking, "Little compared to what?" Encourage students to identify shape, size, color, and material. Repeat this activity with many different objects until students become fluent with the concept of knowledge. You will be pleasantly surprised by the quality of responses. You should be able to brainstorm three or four objects in a ten-minute period.

Other Knowledge Ideas

Have students list all the facts they can about the following things.

• dogs	• cats	• cars
• boats	• planes	• horses
• TV	• Mars	• school
• rules	• clowns	• modeling clay

2 Teaching Comprehension

Comprehension is very similar to knowledge. It is more than just knowing the facts; it is understanding purpose or meaning. Following the procedure used with knowledge, pick an object out of the Thinking Box. Ask the class to think of as many uses as they can for the object. After a minute or two, let the class share responses while you record them. Encourage creative answers. Once, when sharing answers about a marking pen, one student shared that "You could kill a bug with it," and another shared that "You could draw fake blood on your face with it." The key concept here is to get students to stretch themselves when thinking of different uses for these objects so that they understand as much as they can about each object.

Other Comprehension Ideas

Have students explain the different uses of these things.

• pets	• clowns	• an amusement park
• football	• the beach	• plants
• dodge ball	• school	• posters
• dinner	• tools	• crayons

3 Teaching Application

Application is doing; it is using objects or knowledge. To have students practice applying knowledge, hand four or five items from the Thinking Box to different students, and ask them to demonstrate the objects' uses. Students might use a ball for a game of catch or a ruler to draw a straight line. After each student has shared, pass the same objects to other students and have them demonstrate different uses for the objects. Students will enjoy thinking of new ways of using objects—they might even begin to do some synthesis!

Other Application Ideas

Have students demonstrate or explain the following.

- how to play a game
- how to use a marker
- how to write a sentence
- how to clean a desk
- how to make a mess
- how to shoot a basket
- how to set a table
- how to be a friend

4 Teaching Analysis

After practicing knowledge, comprehension, and application, students can practice analysis. The better they can do the first three, the better they can analyze. Explain to your students that *analysis* is the ability to recognize similarities and differences, to compare. A Venn diagram is a great tool for this, but do this activity with a simple chart before you do it with a Venn diagram.

Draw a line down the middle of a chart. Label one column *Alike* and the other column *Different*. Hold up two objects from the box at the same time. First have students share similarities between the two objects while you list them; then have the students share differences. Students will soon learn that the more knowledge, comprehension, and application they have about the objects, the more comparisons they will be able to make. Start with simple items and then use items that really seem to have no apparent similarities or differences. When students become good at this, you can introduce the Venn diagram and have students list unique attributes of each object, as well as similar attributes.

Another way to practice analysis is to have students list the many parts of an object or describe the steps necessary to make or take apart an object.

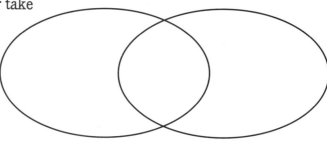

Venn Diagram

Other Analysis Ideas

As a class, compare the following thiings.

- a bathtub and the ocean
- an amusement park and a farm
- boats and airplanes
- how to make a mess
- singing and yelling
- motorcycles and cars

5 Teaching Synthesis

Synthesis is the ability to put together parts to create or make something new. It is also the ability to combine objects or ideas in new and useful ways. Have students practice this skill by giving them two or three objects at the same time. Then ask them to make or do something, using the objects together. They might use a piece of string and a pencil to draw a circle, or a ball and a ruler to invent a new game. At the beginning, give students objects that can easily be combined; but, after practice, choose objects that really cause them to stretch their creative-thinking skills.

Students can also practice synthesis through art. List three or four items on the board. Ask students to draw pictures that include all the items in ways that make sense. An example of this would be to have each student draw a picture that includes a ball, a boat, a tree, and a truck.

These synthesis activities enable students to begin to see relationships between objects and ideas in different ways and from different points of view.

Other Synthesis Ideas

- Write a recipe for happiness, friendship, or fear.
- Design a better school desk.
- Invent a new game to play at school.
- Create a better way to organize the classroom.
- Make a paper airplane that flies straight.

6 Teaching Evaluation

Evaluation is the ability to make and support decisions and judgments. Fluency in the other levels of the taxonomy greatly improves a student's ability to evaluate.

A simple process can be used to teach students to consider all factors when making an evaluation. Divide a chart down the middle. Label one column *Pluses* and the other *Minuses*. The pluses are the good things about an object or position, or the things that seem to support a decision. The minuses are the things that are bad, or contrary to a position or decision. Choose an object from the Thinking Box and have students brainstorm the pluses (good things) about the object and the minuses (bad things) about the object.

The following example shows the pluses and minuses of a flashlight.

Pluses	Minuses
It's portable.	The batteries go dead.
It provides light.	It breaks if you drop it.
You can find things at night.	It's too big for your pocket.
You can use it camping.	It's an ugly color.
You can use it as a weapon to protect yourself.	

This process may not seem significant or important when used in examples like these but, once learned, it can be used to compare and process information about more difficult decisions.

Other Evaluation Ideas

Do a pluses-and-minuses chart for the following.

- a bike
- a car
- ice cream
- walking home from school
- eating a school lunch
- cold days

- a motorcycle
- a truck
- frozen yogurt
- riding the bus
- bringing lunch
- hot days

Dog Dilemma
or
Cat Taskgraphy?

PART I

Information Gathering and Processing

Student Reproducibles

PART II

Writing the Persuasive Paper and Using the Writing Templates

Student Reproducibles

Dog Dilemma or Cat Taskgraphy?

Introduction

The object of this lesson is for students to use a variety of thinking skills to make and support a decision about which pet is better. The lesson concludes with students writing a persuasive essay to support their decision.

This Sequential Thinking Lesson can be done with all grade levels. It uses fairly concrete subjects and ideas that enable students to generate and process a great deal of information. Part I of the lesson uses taxonomy to gather and process information. It is designed to be done in cooperative groups or as a whole class. Each activity has student recording guides following the teacher directions. Part II of the lesson has students use one of three writing templates to generate a persuasive position paper. Directions for using the templates begin on page 25. Part II should be completed individually.

- Estimated time: 3 to 5 hours over 3 to 5 days

- Curriculum knowledge needed by students: None

Role of the Teacher

The role of the teacher in this and all Sequential Lessons is that of a facilitator. If students have practiced the thinking taxonomy and are comfortable with the levels of the taxonomy, Part I will be simple. If they have not done much work with the thinking taxonomy, the teacher will have to provide more direction. Part I has six activities. The teacher should introduce each activity. After introducing the activity, give one or two examples to get the groups started. Once groups have started, move from group to group, encouraging expansive and creative thought.

HINT: During this and other sequential lessons, primary teachers may choose to do all or most of the activities as a whole group, with the teacher being the recorder. Intermediate and middle-school teachers will want students to work in groups with guidance from the teacher.

PART I: Information Gathering and Processing

Introduce the lesson by asking, "Which is a better pet, a cat or a dog?" At this point, most students will have an opinion—but they will not be able to defend their position or convince others that their choice is the best. The purpose of the next few activities is to gather enough information to support their opinions in a way that will persuade others to think as they do.

If the lesson is being done in groups, each group should have a copy of the recording guides (see pages 21–24) to complete as they go through each activity. If the lesson is being done as a whole class, the teacher can do all the recording, or students can copy the teacher's recording. Prewriters should not be asked to keep recording guides because it will frustrate their thinking.

Activity 1 Knowledge

The object of Activity 1 is to gather as much knowledge as possible about cats and dogs. If students are doing this lesson as a whole group, make a chart or an overhead similar to the student recording guides. Charts are preferable because they can be left on display during the lesson. An overhead or a simple chart on the board can be used to give a few examples to get students started.

Activity 1 *(Example)*

Dog	Cat
It's a mammal.	It's furry.
It's loyal.	It meows.
It barks.	It likes to play with string.

Activity 2   Comprehension

The object of Activity 2 is to gain better comprehension of what a pet really is. In groups or as a whole class, students discuss what a pet is and then, either in their groups or individually, write one sentence that would explain to someone from another planet what a pet is.

Activity 2 *(Example)*

A pet is an animal that is fun to be around, plays with you, protects you, and depends on you for its food and water.

Activity 3   Application

The object of Activity 3 is to give students the feeling of the responsibility of owning a pet. In groups or as a whole class, students list as many responsibilities involved in owning a pet as they can. A good way to enhance this part of the lesson is to bring in guest speakers who own pets. Most cities have Humane Societies, whose members love to visit schools to talk about pet care. Parents can also bring in pets and talk about the responsibility of owning a pet. Another option is to have a classroom pet and share with the class the responsibility of caring for the pet.

Activity 3 *(Example)*

You must feed it, love it, play with it, make sure it gets exercise, bathe it, clean up after it, make sure it has a place to sleep, teach it how to behave, take care of it when it is sick, take it to the vet, get it shots, buy it a collar and toys, buy food . . . .

Activity 4   Analysis

The object of Activity 4 is to decide how the two pets are alike and how they are different. In this case, students will be considering the similarities and differences between dogs and cats. This lesson includes a simple table as a student recording guide to list similarities and differences.

Activity 4 *(Example)*

Alike	Different
Both have claws.	They make different sounds.
Both are furry.	Some dogs are bigger.
Both have fleas.	Dogs can be trained to protect.

Activity 5 Synthesis

The object of Activity 5 is to have students imagine the perfect pet. By considering the perfect pet, they can compare both the dog and the cat to their creation to see which is closer to their ideal. It is important for the teacher to encourage creativity in this part of the lesson. Remind students that this is their own creation and that there are no limits. The activity asks students, either in groups or individually, to draw and label their perfect pets. It is important that students label their drawings in a way that explains why their pets are perfect.

Activity 5 *(Example)*

Here is a description of one student's perfect pet.

It would never need to be fed, it could change from a dog to a horse, it would always love you, it would not die until after you did, it would not need to go to the bathroom, it would be very smart and talented.

Activity 6 Evaluation

The object of Activity 6 is for students to begin evaluating the merits of the information that they have processed up to this point. By now, students should have a pretty good understanding of the similarities and differences between the two pets (knowing the similarities and differences requires an understanding of the knowledge, comprehension, and application of the information). The synthesis activity helped students consider what they would really like in a pet, if given their choice. Now it is time to evaluate the two pets based on all this information. To do this, students do a pluses-and-minuses chart for both the dog and the cat.

Completing the Evaluation Activity in groups helps balance the opinions and improves the chance of students' considering all factors before making their choices. Students complete the charts, and then they are ready to use that information to write their persuasive papers.

Activity 6 *(Example)*

Pluses of a Dog	Minuses of a Dog
It can protect you.	It makes a mess in the yard.
It can chase a Frisbee.	It needs a big yard.
It is loyal.	It barks.

PART II: Writing the Persuasive Paper

NOTE: *Directions for writing the persuasive paper and using the writing templates begin on page 25.*

Dog Dilemma or Cat Taskgraphy?

Knowledge

Write as many facts about cats and dogs as your group can think of.

Cats	Dogs

Comprehension

Discuss in your group what a pet is. After a few minutes, see if you can write one sentence that would explain pets to someone from another planet who has no idea what a pet is.

_____

_____

_____

_____

_____

_____

Application

List as many responsibilities of owning a pet as you can think of.

_____

_____

_____

_____

_____

_____

_____

_____

Analysis

Compare dogs and cats. How are they alike and how are they different?

Alike	Different

Synthesis

After discussing a perfect pet with members of your group, invent what would be a perfect pet for you. Draw and label your pet, describe your pet with a list, or write a story telling about your perfect pet. Be creative! (You may use the back of this page, too.)

Evaluation

Write the pluses and minuses about dogs, and then write the
pluses and minuses about cats.

Pluses About Dogs	Minuses About Dogs

Pluses About Cats	Minuses About Cats

Writing the Persuasive Paper
and
Using the Writing Templates

Once students have worked together to gather and process the information in Part I of the lesson, they are ready to choose a position and logically present their argument. Lead students through the following steps, using the template and directions that are appropriate for their level. Young students and beginning writers who are not ready to do this activity independently can do it orally with the teacher.

While students are completing the template, it is important that teachers stay on top of things. Students have generated an abundance of good information, analysis, and evaluations up to this point. Make sure that they use this information in their writing.

If Part I was done as a whole group, then the charts should be left up so students can have access to the information. If Part I was done in small groups, it might be helpful to make copies of group work for members of the group so that they have notes to refer to while writing. After students complete the template, they can edit and then recopy or type their final paper. It may be enough just to have beginning writers complete the template. Teachers may want to keep students together the first few times the template is used to make sure that students understand the process of writing a persuasive paper.

The
Beginning Writer Template

The teacher should lead beginning writers through the template. It might be helpful to do a class paper together as a model before students complete their own.

Step 1   **Select an Audience**

Students should decide who they are trying to convince— another classmate, Mom and Dad, the principal, or a person from another planet. Do this to get students thinking about writing for different audiences. It may not change what or how they write at this point, but it may in the future.

Step 2   **State a Position**

Each student should choose a position and complete the first sentence, called a thesis statement. Explain to students that this is where they tell the audience what they think.

Step 3   **Paragraph 1**

Each student writes a sentence stating three reasons that support his or her position.

Steps 4–6   **Paragraphs 2–4**

In these three steps the writer restates each reason and writes one good sentence to support each reason.

Step 7   **Paragraph 5**

To conclude the paper, each student should try to write a sentence that states why his or her position is best and why it is important.

Beginning Writer Sample
from
"Dog Dilemma or Cat Taskgraphy?"

I think a dog is a better pet than a cat. Dogs protect you, they are loyal, and they play with you.

One reason why dogs are better than cats is because they protect you. Dogs can be trained to protect you and keep bad people away from your house.

Another reason why dogs are better than cats is because they are loyal. Dogs love their owners and always stay with them and follow them.

A last reason dogs are better than cats is because they play with you. My dog chases a ball and jumps in the swimming pool.

I think you should buy a dog for a pet because they are fun and can protect you better than a cat.

by Timmy H., age 8

The
Intermediate Writer Template

At this stage the teacher might work through the first few steps with the students before they work independently.

Step 1   **Select an Audience**
Students should decide who they are trying to convince—another classmate, Mom and Dad, the principal, or a person from another planet. Do this to get students thinking about writing for different audiences. It may not change what or how they write at this point, but it may in the future.

Step 2   **Paragraph 1**
Each student should choose a position and write a thesis statement that states the position. Explain to students that this is where they tell the audience what they think. Next, each student should write three sentences that give different reasons that support his or her position.

Step 3   **Paragraphs 2–4**
Paragraphs 2–4 each start with a restatement of one of the reasons given in paragraph 1. After restating the reason, two to five sentences are written to support each reason. Support sentences can present a logical argument, state a philosophical position, or appeal to emotions. Some students choose to cite research or tell a brief story that supports the reason. Good writers will use a variety of different approaches to present their arguments.

Step 4   **Paragraph 5**
Paragraph 5 brings closure to the argument. It should restate the position, summarize the argument, and attempt to answer these questions: So what? Why is the position important? In the case of the cat-or-dog position paper, the writer may imply that choosing the best pet is important to make sure that the pet gets a home where it will be properly cared for.

Intermediate Writer Sample
from
"Dog Dilemma or Cat Taskgraphy?"

I think that a cat is a better pet than a dog. Cats know where to go to the bathroom. They keep themselves very clean. Cats also can live in an apartment.

It is important that pets know where to go to the bathroom. This makes sure they do not ruin the carpet. Cats can be trained to use a kitty box. Felines never make a mess in the yard.

Cats keep themselves very clean. One thing cats do that dogs don't is wash themselves. This means that you do not have to give them a bath. Cats don't smell like dogs do when they are dirty.

I live in an apartment, so it is important that cats do not need a yard. Cats can climb fences and wander around to get exercise. Cats do not need a fenced yard to keep them from running away. They always come back when they go out.

Cats make better pets than dogs because they are easier to care for and do not need a big yard. It is important to choose a cat for a pet if you live in an apartment or if you do not like to give it a bath or clean up. I think you should buy a cat for those reasons.

by Joy V., age 11

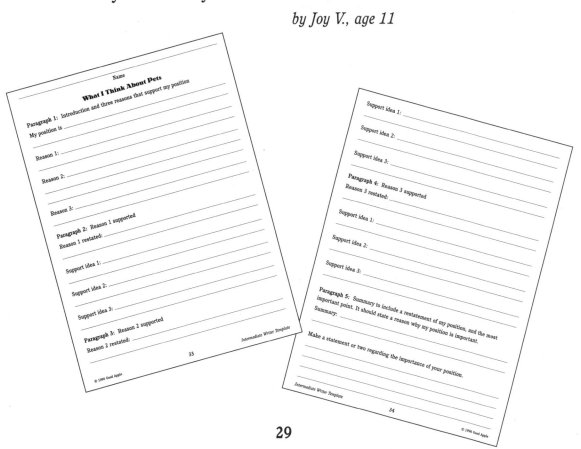

The
Advanced Writer Template

By this stage, writers are able to progress through the template on their own.

Step 1 **Select an Audience**

Students should decide who they are trying to convince—another classmate, Mom and Dad, the principal, a person from another planet. Do this to get students thinking about writing for different audiences. It may not change what or how they write at this point, but it may in the future.

Step 2 **Paragraph 1**

Whenever possible, advanced writers should use an attention-getting technique to introduce their position. This can be done with a startling fact, a quote from a famous person, a research fact, or a humorous or interesting anecdote. After the opening the advanced writer should write a thesis statement that clearly states his or her position. Three to five reasons should follow the thesis statement.

Step 3 **Middle Paragraphs (3–5)**

After restating the reason, several sentences are written to support each reason. Support sentences can present a logical argument, state a philosophical position, or appeal to emotions. Some students may choose to cite research or tell a brief story that supports the reason. Good writers will use a variety of different approaches to present their arguments. Advanced writers might also choose to consider a point from another position, support it, and then refute the argument. Advanced writers also make extensive use of examples to make their point. These two strategies add the appearance of firsthand knowledge and establish the writer as an expert on the topic.

Step 4   Closing Paragraph

The closing paragraph brings closure to the argument. It should restate the position, summarize the argument, and attempt to answer these questions: So what? Why is the position important? Advanced writers may again choose to use an example or to refute the opposite position in the closing paragraph.

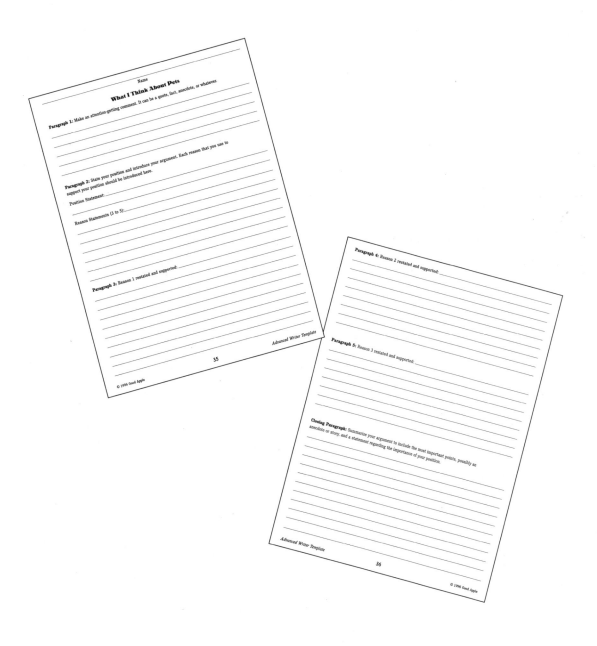

Name

What I Think About Pets

I think a _____ is a better pet than a _____

Three reasons I think this are _____

_____

_____

_____

• One reason I think this is _____

_____

I know this because _____

_____

• The second reason I know this is _____

_____

This is true because _____

_____

• The last reason I think this is _____

_____

I know this because _____

_____

I think you should get a _____ instead of a _____

because _____

_____

_____

_____

_____

Name

What I Think About Pets

Paragraph 1: Introduction and three reasons that support my position

My position is _____

_____

Reason 1: _____

_____

Reason 2: _____

_____

_____

Reason 3: _____

_____

Paragraph 2: Reason 1 supported

Reason 1 restated: _____

_____

Support idea 1: _____

_____

Support idea 2: _____

_____

Support idea 3: _____

_____

Paragraph 3: Reason 2 supported

Reason 2 restated: _____

_____

Support idea 1: _____

_____

Support idea 2: _____

_____

Support idea 3: _____

_____

Paragraph 4: Reason 3 supported

Reason 3 restated: _____

_____

Support idea 1: _____

_____

Support idea 2: _____

_____

Support idea 3: _____

_____

Paragraph 5: Summary to include a restatement of my position, and the most important point. It should state a reason why my position is important.

Summary: _____

_____

Make a statement or two regarding the importance of your position.

_____

_____

_____

_____

Name

What I Think About Pets

Paragraph 1: Make an attention-getting comment. It can be a quote, fact, anecdote . . .

_____

_____

_____

_____

Paragraph 2: State your position and introduce your argument. Each reason that you use to support your position should be introduced here.

Position Statement: _____

_____

Reason Statements (3 to 5) _____

_____

_____

_____

_____

_____

Paragraph 3: Reason 1 restated and supported _____

_____

_____

_____

_____

_____

_____

_____

_____

Advanced Writer Template

Paragraph 4: Reason 2 restated and supported _____

_____

_____

_____

_____

_____

_____

Paragraph 5: Reason 3 restated and supported _____

_____

_____

_____

_____

_____

_____

Closing Paragraph: Summarize your argument to include the most important points, possibly an anecdote or story, and a statement of importance of your position.

_____

_____

_____

_____

_____

_____

_____

_____

_____

Teaching Persuasive Writing

Teaching Persuasive Writing

Using Thinking Skills to Prove Your Point

Persuasive writing requires students to choose a position, make judgments and evaluations, offer proposals, and argue convincingly for their position.

After completing the Sequential Lesson, the writing templates provide students with guides to generate and organize their thinking into clear and concise arguments. Some students may choose to examine and support only one side of an issue; others may explore both sides of an issue and then offer a compromise or alternate solution. Effective writers use quotes, examples, anecdotes, and specific evidence to support their positions. Convincing arguments may appeal to facts and logic, emotions,* or philosophical beliefs. Many great writers follow this simple formula.

Start by telling the readers what you think. Next, explain why you think what you think. Finally, remind them what you think. This strategy is used in debates, speeches, and written position papers. Persuasive writers establish in their writing that they are informed and knowledgeable about their subject. They give background information to focus their writing. It is also important that persuasive writers consider their audience. Writing to the school principal might be reason to rely on facts and logical persuasion, while appealing to classmates might be reason to rely more on emotions and philosophical beliefs. Systematic development of a position is important throughout the persuasive argument. The following few pages provide step-by-step directions for writing an effective persuasive paper.

*Appealing to emotions is not generally considered an effective strategy in a persuasive argument. However, the State of California does list appealing to emotions as an effective persuasive method in its scoring rubrics.

Organizing the Paper

First Paragraph

The first paragraph of a position paper generally makes a statement of position (thesis statement). In many cases, a startling statement or quote is used to get the reader's attention and make the position seem logical and worthy of consideration. The position is then clearly stated and followed by several reasons, facts, concepts, or ideas that support the position.

Middle Paragraphs

The middle paragraphs each take one of the supporting ideas and expand on it. Ideas can be supported by facts, examples, testimony of experts, research data, and speculation. Avoiding evidence of personal bias and statements of personal opinion add strength to the position.

Closing Paragraph

The final paragraph summarizes the ideas and then restates the position in an even more convincing manner.

It is critical that a position be selected on merit and belief, not on impulse or peer pressure. Considering the following points will help the writer choose a position that can be supported.

1. Thoroughly examine all sides of the issue.

2. Know the facts.

3. Know how the facts can be used to support other positions.

4. Know the similarities and differences in positions.

5. Consider alternatives and compromises.

6. Know the pluses and minuses about all sides of the issue.

Each Sequential Lesson includes a template for the beginning and intermediate writer that has been modified for that lesson. Advanced writers should use the Advanced Writer Template, on pages 159–160.

> **NOTE:** *Even though the template was designed specifically for persuasive writing, it also can be used for expressive writing that asks students to reflect on their ideas or opinions about certain topics. The template will help students organize their thoughts and present them in a logical manner.*

You will also find at the back of the book two generic prewriting reproducibles designed to encourage critical thinking about issues, ideas, positions, and opinions. They are appropriate to use before doing persuasive, evaluative, or problem-solution writing.

The Sequential Lessons

Which Playground Ball Is Best?

Introduction

The object of this lesson is for students to use a variety of thinking skills to make and support a decision about playground balls. The lesson concludes with students writing a persuasive essay to support their decision.

This Sequential Thinking Lesson can be done with all grade levels. It uses playground balls, well known to all students, as concrete objects that enable students to generate and process a great deal of information. Part I of the lesson uses the taxonomy to gather and process information. It is designed to be done in cooperative groups or as a whole class. Each activity has student recording guides following the teacher directions. Part II of the lesson has students use one of three writing templates to generate a persuasive position paper. Directions for using the templates begin on page 25. Part II should be completed individually.

- Estimated time: 3 to 5 hours over 3 to 5 days

- Curriculum knowledge needed by students: None

Role of the Teacher

The role of the teacher in this and all Sequential Lessons is that of a facilitator. If students have practiced the thinking taxonomy and are comfortable with the levels of the taxonomy, Part I will be simple. If they have not done much work with the thinking taxonomy, the teacher will have to provide more direction. Part I has six activities. The teacher should introduce each activity. After introducing the activity, give one or two examples to get the groups started. Once groups are started, move from group to group, encouraging expansive and creative thought.

PART I: Information Gathering and Processing

Introduce the lesson by asking, "Which is a better ball, a red ball or a soccer ball?" At this point, most students will have an opinion—but they will not be able to defend their position or convince others that their choice is the best. The purpose of the next few activities is to gather enough information to support their opinions in a way that will persuade others to think as they do. If you need help with the lesson design, see the directions for the "Dog Dilemma or Cat Taskgraphy?" lesson.

If the lesson is being done in groups, each group should have a copy of the recording guides to complete as they go through each activity. If the lesson is being done as a whole class, the teacher can do all the recording, or students can copy the teacher recording.

Activity 1 Knowledge

Allow students to touch and feel each ball. Next let them generate a list describing each ball.

Activity 1 *(Example)*

Red Ball	Soccer Ball
It's red.	It's hard.
It bounces high.	It lasts a long time.
It is hard to catch.	It is easy to throw.

Activity 2 Comprehension

To demonstrate a better understanding of the attributes of each ball, each group will write two or three sentences describing each ball.

Activity 2 *(Example)*

Red balls are soft; they don't hurt when you catch them; and they pop easily. We aren't supposed to kick them, either.

Soccer balls are hard and for soccer. They last a long time and should just be used for soccer.

Activity 3   Application

Have students generate a list of uses for each ball and put a star by three uses that their group thinks are the best. A good integrated physical-education lesson is to go out with red balls and soccer balls and let groups try different games with each ball for comparison.

Activity 3 *(Example)*

Red Ball Uses	Soccer Ball Uses
Dodge ball	Soccer
Hand ball	Kick ball
Catch	Catch

Activity 4   Analysis

Have each group compare the two balls. How are they alike and how are they different?

Activity 4 *(Example)*

How are they alike?	How are they different?
Both are round.	One is hard; one is soft.
Both bounce.	They're different colors.
They hold air.	Soccer ball hurts.

Activity 5   Synthesis

In this activity, students will create the perfect playground ball. Start by having each group brainstorm a few qualities the perfect ball might have. Next have students draw and label the perfect ball. This activity can be done in groups, but you may want to have each student draw and label his or her own ball after a group discussion.

Activity 5 *(Example)*

The perfect ball doesn't hurt when it hits you; it never goes flat; it comes back when you miss it or when it goes over the fence;

it never goes on the roof; the room number never comes off; and it goes where you want it to when you throw it.

Activity 6 Evaluation

Have each group complete the pluses-and-minuses chart. Make sure that students refer to the information gathered in the first five activities.

Activity 6 *(Example)*

Pluses of red ball	Minuses of red ball
It doesn't hurt.	It pops easily.
It is great for dodge ball.	You can't kick it.
It is good for little kids.	Room number comes off, and you lose it.

PART II: Writing the Persuasive Paper

NOTE: Directions for writing the persuasive paper and using the writing templates begin on page 25.

Which Playground Ball Is Best?

Knowledge

Write as many facts about red balls and soccer balls as your group can think of.

Red Balls	Soccer Balls

Activity 2

Comprehension

Discuss the two balls in your group. After a few minutes, write two or three sentences describing each ball.

Application

List as many uses for each ball as you can think of.

Red Ball	Soccer Ball

Analysis

Compare the two balls. How are they alike and how are they different?

Alike	Different

Synthesis

After discussing a perfect ball with members of your group, invent what would be a perfect ball for you. Draw and label your ball, or describe it with a list. Be creative!

© 1996 Good Apple

Evaluation

Write the pluses and minuses about red balls. Then write the pluses and minuses about soccer balls.

Pluses About Red Balls	Minuses About Red Balls

Pluses About Soccer Balls	Minuses About Soccer Balls

© 1996 Good Apple   **49**   *Activity 6*

Name _____

Which Playground Ball Is Best?

I think a _____ is a better ball than a _____

Three reasons I think this are _____

_____

_____

• One reason I think this is _____

_____

I know this because _____

_____

• The second reason I think this is _____

_____

This is true because _____

_____

• The last reason I think this is _____

I know this because _____

_____

I think we should have more _____ balls than _____

balls because _____

_____

_____

_____

_____

Name

Which Playground Ball Is Best?

Paragraph 1: Introduction and three reasons that support my position

I think a _____ is a better ball than a _____

The first reason I think this is _____

_____

The second reason is _____

_____

The third reason is _____

_____

Paragraph 2: Reason 1 supported

Reason 1 restated: _____

_____

Support idea 1: _____

_____

Support idea 2: _____

_____

Support idea 3: _____

_____

Paragraph 3: Reason 2 supported

Reason 2 restated: _____

_____

Support idea 1: _____

_____

Support idea 2: _____

_____

Support idea 3: _____

_____

Paragraph 4: Reason 3 supported

Reason 3 restated: _____

_____

Support idea 1: _____

_____

Support idea 2: _____

_____

Support idea 3: _____

_____

Paragraph 5: Summary

Restate position with most important point. _____

_____

Make a statement or two regarding the importance of your position. _____

_____

_____

_____

Pen or Pencil?

Introduction

The object of this lesson is for students to use a variety of thinking skills to make and support a decision about writing tools. The lesson concludes with students writing a persuasive essay to support their decision.

This Sequential Thinking Lesson can be done with all grade levels. It uses a pen and a pencil, well known to all students, as concrete objects that enable students to generate and process a great deal of information. Part I of the lesson uses the taxonomy to gather and process information. It is designed to be done in cooperative groups or as a whole class. Each activity has student recording guides following the teacher directions. Part II of the lesson has students use one of three writing templates to generate a persuasive position paper. Directions for using the templates begin on page 25. Part II should be completed individually.

- Estimated time: 3 to 5 hours over 3 to 5 days

- Curriculum knowledge needed by students: None

Role of the Teacher

The role of the teacher in this and all Sequential Lessons is that of a facilitator. If students have practiced the thinking taxonomy and are comfortable with the levels of the taxonomy, Part I will be simple. If they have not done much work with the thinking taxonomy, the teacher will have to provide more direction. Part I has six activities. The teacher should introduce each activity. After introducing the activity, give one or two examples to get the groups started. Once groups have started, move from group to group, encouraging expansive and creative thought.

PART I: Information Gathering and Processing

Introduce the lesson by asking, "Which is a better writing tool, a pen or a pencil?" At this point, most students will have an opinion—but they will not be able to defend their position or convince others that their choice is the best. The students' purpose is to gather enough information to support their opinions in a way that will persuade others to think as they do. If you need help with the lesson design, see the directions for the "Dog Dilemma or Cat Taskgraphy?" lesson.

If the lesson is being done in groups, each group should have a copy of the recording guides to complete as they go through each activity. If the lesson is being done as a whole class, the teacher can do all the recording, or students can copy the teacher recording. Prewriters should not be asked to keep recording guides because it will frustrate their thinking.

Activity 1 Knowledge

Groups generate a list of facts about each writing tool.

Activity 1 *(Example)*

Pen	Pencil
Smears	Have to sharpen it
Many colors	Erasable
Permanent	Breaks easily

Activity 2 Comprehension

To demonstrate a better understanding of the attributes of each writing tool, have groups write two or three sentences describing each.

Activity 2 *(Example)*

Pencils have to be sharpened, and they break easily. Sometimes you have to use them to take tests. They are good to draw with.

Pens are hard to write with if you make mistakes. Never do math with pens. Erasable pens are neat, but they smear.

Activity 3 Application

Have students generate a list of uses for each writing tool and put a star by their three favorite uses. Have them write the pen list with a pen and the pencil list with a pencil.

Activity 3 *(Example)*

Pencil Uses	Pen Uses
Sketching	Writing stories
Great for math	Outlining drawings
Shading	Correcting

Activity 4 Analysis

Have each group compare the two writing tools. How are they alike and how are they different?

Activity 4 *(Example)*

How are they alike?	How are they different?
Both are round.	One is hard; one is soft.
Both write.	They come in different colors.
Both have different colors	Pencils erase easily.

Activity 5 Synthesis

In this activity, students will design the perfect writing tool. They will discuss the qualities of the perfect writing tool and then draw and label their own tool. Remind them to tell all that their tool will do.

Activity 5 *(Example)*

The perfect writing tool is easy to erase, it changes colors, never makes spelling mistakes, and never needs to be erased.

Activity 6   Evaluation

Have each group complete the pluses-and-minuses chart. Make sure that students refer to the information gathered in the first five activities.

Activity 6 *(Example)*

Pluses of a Pencil	Minuses of a Pencil
It is erasable.	It breaks.
It doesn't cost a lot.	It makes a mess when you erase.
It is easy to use.	It wears down too fast.

PART II: Writing the Persuasive Paper

NOTE: *Directions for writing the persuasive paper and using the writing templates begin on page 25.*

Pen or Pencil?

Knowledge

Write as many facts about pencils and pens as your group can think of.

Pencils	Pens

Comprehension

Discuss the two writing tools in your group. After a few minutes, write two or three sentences describing each tool.

Activity 3

Application

List as many uses for each tool as you can.

Pencils	Pens

Activity 4

Analysis

Compare the two writing tools. How are they alike and how are they different?

Alike	Different

Synthesis

After discussing a perfect writing tool with members of your group, invent what would be a perfect writing tool for you. Draw and label your writing tool, or draw it and describe it with a list. Be creative!

Evaluation

Write the pluses and minuses about pencils, and then write the
pluses and minuses about pens.

Pluses About Pencils	Minuses About Pencils

Pluses About Pens	Minuses About Pens

　　　　© 1996 Good Apple

Name

Pen or Pencil?

I think a _____ is a better writing tool than a _____

Three reasons I think this are _____

_____

_____

• One reason I think this is _____

_____

I know this because _____

• The second reason I think this is _____

_____

This is true because _____

_____

• The last reason I think this is _____
I know this because _____

_____

I think we should use _____ instead of _____

because _____

_____

_____

_____

_____

Name

Pen or Pencil?

Paragraph 1: Introduction and three reasons that support my position

I think a _____ is a better writing tool than a _____

The first reason I think this is _____

_____

The second reason is _____

_____

The third reason is _____

_____

Paragraph 2: Reason 1 supported

Reason 1 restated: _____

_____

Support idea 1: _____

_____

Support idea 2: _____

_____

Support idea 3: _____

_____

Paragraph 3: Reason 2 supported

Reason 2 restated: _____

_____

Support idea 1: _____

_____

Support idea 2: _____

_____

Support idea 3: _____

_____

Paragraph 4: Reason 3 supported

Reason 3 restated: _____

_____

Support idea 1: _____

_____

Support idea 2: _____

_____

Support idea 3: _____

_____

Paragraph 5: Summary

Restate position with most important point. _____

_____

Make a statement or two regarding the importance of your position. _____

_____

_____

_____

_____

A Trip to the Beach or a Day at the Pool?

Introduction

The object of this lesson is for students to use a variety of thinking skills to make and support a decision about where to spend a day. The lesson concludes with students writing a persuasive essay to support their decision.

This Sequential Thinking Lesson can be done with all grade levels. It uses going to the beach or going to the pool as ideas that enable students to generate and process a great deal of information. Part I of the lesson uses the taxonomy to gather and process information. It is designed to be done in cooperative groups or as a whole class. Each activity has student recording guides following the teacher directions. Part II of the lesson has students use one of three writing templates to generate a persuasive position paper. Directions for using the templates begin on page 25. Part II should be completed individually.

- Estimated time: 3 to 5 hours over 3 to 5 days

- Curriculum knowledge needed by students: None

Role of the Teacher

The role of the teacher in this and all Sequential Lessons is that of a facilitator. If students have practiced the thinking taxonomy and are comfortable with the levels of the taxonomy, Part I will be simple. If they have not done much work with the thinking taxonomy, the teacher will have to provide more direction. Part I has six activities. The teacher should introduce each activity. After introducing the activity, give one or two examples to get the groups started. Once groups have started, move from group to group, encouraging expansive and creative thought.

PART I: Information Gathering and Processing

Introduce the lesson by asking, "Which is more fun, going to the pool or to the beach?" *This lesson can be easily modified by comparing two other locations, such as the park or the mountains, water skiing or snow skiing.* At this point, most students will have an opinion—but they will not be able to defend their position or convince others that their choice is the best. The students' purpose is to gather enough information to support their opinions in a way that will persuade others to think as they do. If you need help with the lesson design, see the directions for the "Dog Dilemma or Cat Taskgraphy?" lesson.

If the lesson is being done in groups, each group should have a copy of the recording guides to complete as they go through each activity. If the lesson is being done as a whole class, the teacher can do all the recording or students can copy the teacher recording.

Activity 1 Knowledge

Groups generate a list of facts about each place.

Activity 1 *(Example)*

The Pool	The Beach
Diving board	Sand
Clear water	Waves
No running	Fish

Activity 2 Comprehension

To demonstrate a better understanding of the attributes of each place, have groups write two or three sentences describing each.

Activity 2 *(Example)*

The pool is a place where you can go with your friends. The water is warm, and there is a diving board.

The beach has sand and waves. You can play in the water or in the sand.

Activity 3 Application

Have students generate a list of activities that can be done at each location.

Activity 3 *(Example)*

Pool	Beach
Diving	Surfing
Swimming laps	Building castles
Playing Marco Polo	Fishing

Activity 4 Analysis

Have each group compare the two locations. How are they alike and how are they different?

How are they alike?	How are they different?
Both have water.	The beach has sand.
Both are fun.	There are waves.
You can use toys.	Water temperature

Activity 5 Synthesis

In this activity, students will plan a day at the pool and a day at the beach. They should plan all the different activities and games they will play, as well as transportation, lunch, and parking.

Activity 5 *(Example)*

We will take the bus to the pool, so parking is not a problem. We will all take fifty cents to get in. They don't have food there, so we have to bring lunch. They sell drinks, so we will bring sandwiches, chips, and cookies. When we get there, we will just play a little to get used to it. Then we will play tag and Marco Polo. We will also spend time on the diving board. We want to take a raft and a ball to play with. When we get tired, we will rest and eat lunch. Then we will play some more. We also want to practice our swimming strokes.

Activity 6 Evaluation

Have each group complete the pluses-and-minuses chart. Make sure that students refer to the information gathered in the first five activities.

Activity 6 *(Example)*

Pluses About the Beach	Minuses About the Beach
Waves	You have to walk far.
It's free.	The water is cold.
Building sand castles	Seaweed and jelly fish

PART II: Writing the Persuasive Paper

NOTE: Directions for writing the persuasive paper and using the writing templates begin on page 25.

A Trip to the Beach or a Day at the Pool?

Knowledge

Write as many facts about the pool and the beach as your group can think of.

Pool	Beach

Activity 2

Comprehension

Discuss the two swimming places. After a few minutes, write two or three sentences describing each.

Application

List things you can do at each place.

Pool	Beach

Analysis

Compare the two places. How are they alike and how are they different?

Alike	Different

Synthesis

Discuss in your group what you would do at the beach and at the pool. Plan a day at each. Include how you would get there, parking, lunch, and the activities you would do.

A Day at the Pool	A Day at the Beach

Evaluation

Write the pluses and minuses about the pool and the beach.

Pluses About the Pool	Minuses About the Pool

Pluses About the Beach	Minuses About the Beach

© 1996 Good Apple

The Beach or the Pool?

I think going to the _____ is more fun than going to the _____

Three reasons I think this are _____

_____

_____

• One reason I think this is _____

_____

I know this because _____

_____

• The second reason I think this is _____

_____

This is true because _____

_____

• The last reason I think this is _____

_____

I know this because _____

_____

I think we should go to the _____ instead of _____

because _____

_____

_____

_____

_____

Name _____

A Trip to the Beach or a Day at the Pool?

Paragraph 1: Introduction and three reasons that support my position

I think a trip to the _____ would be more fun than a trip to the _____

The first reason I think this is _____

_____

The second reason is _____

_____

The third reason is _____

_____

Paragraph 2: Reason 1 supported

Reason 1 restated: _____

_____

Support idea 1: _____

_____

Support idea 2: _____

_____

Support idea 3: _____

_____

Paragraph 3: Reason 2 supported

Reason 2 restated: _____

_____

Support idea 1: _____

_____

Support idea 2: _____

_____

Support idea 3: _____

_____

Paragraph 4: Reason 3 supported

Reason 3 restated: _____

_____

Support idea 1: _____

_____

Support idea 2: _____

_____

Support idea 3: _____

_____

Paragraph 5: Summary

Restate position with most important point. _____

_____

Make a statement or two regarding the importance of your position. _____

_____

_____

_____

_____

Seeing a Video at Home or Going to the Movies?

Introduction

The object of this lesson is for students to use a variety of thinking skills to make and support a decision about where to watch a movie. The activity concludes with students writing a persuasive essay to support their decision.

This Sequential Thinking Lesson can be done with all grade levels. It uses watching a movie as a concrete activity that enables students to generate and process a great deal of information. Part I of the lesson uses the taxonomy to gather and process information. It is designed to be done in cooperative groups or as a whole class. Each activity has student recording guides following the teacher directions. Part II of the lesson has students use one of three writing templates to generate persuasive position papers. Directions for using the templates begin on page 25. Part II should be completed individually.

- Estimated time: 3 to 5 hours over 3 to 5 days

- Curriculum knowledge needed by students: None

Role of the Teacher

The role of the teacher in this and all Sequential Lessons is that of a facilitator. If students have practiced the thinking taxonomy and are comfortable with the levels of the taxonomy, Part I will be simple. If they have not done much work with the thinking taxonomy, the teacher will have to provide more direction. Part I has six activities. The teacher should introduce each activity. After introducing the activity, give one or two examples to get the groups started. Once groups have started, move from group to group, encouraging expansive and creative thought.

PART I: Information Gathering and Processing

Introduce the lesson by asking, "Which is more fun, going to the movies or watching a video at home?" At this point, most students will have an opinion—but they will not be able to defend their position or convince others that their choice is the best. The purpose of the next few activities is to gather enough information to support their opinions in a way that will persuade others to think as they do. If you need help with the lesson design, see the directions for the "Dog Dilemma or Cat Taskgraphy?" lesson.

If the lesson is being done in groups, each group should have a copy of the recording guides to complete as they go through each activity. If the lesson is being done as a whole class, the teacher can do all the recording, or students can copy the teacher recording.

Activity 1   Knowledge

Groups generate a list of facts about each way of viewing a movie.

Activity 1 *(Example)*

Video at Home	Going to the Movies
Small screen	Crowds
Lots of choices	Expensive food
Low cost	Big screen

Activity 2   Comprehension

To demonstrate a better understanding of the two options, have groups talk about the last time they went to the movies and the last time they watched a video at home. What was the most fun about each? What was the least fun about each? This can be an oral activity, or it can be recorded by each group.

Activity 3   Application

Have half of the groups act out having a good time going to and watching a movie at a theater. Have the other half act out having fun watching a video at home.

Activity 4   Analysis

Compare the experience of going to the movies and watching a video at home.

Activity 4 *(Example)*

How are they alike?	How are they different?
Both have a movie.	The theater is expensive.
Both have food.	There can be disturbances at home.
Both have good movies.	Theater has certain times.

Activity 5   Synthesis

Give each student or group a piece of white construction paper. Let them make a poster advertising their favorite movie. They should include information about the stars and why it is a good movie.

Activity 6   Evaluation

Have each group complete the pluses-and-minuses chart. Make sure that students refer to the information gathered in the first five activities.

Activity 6 *(Example)*

Pluses of a Video	Minuses of a Video
You can pick any movie.	Disturbances
It's cheap.	Screen too small
You can pause.	Only old movies

PART II: Writing the Persuasive Paper

NOTE: Directions for writing the persuasive paper and using the writing templates begin on page 25.

Seeing a Video at Home or Going to the Movies?

Knowledge

Write as many facts as you can about watching a video at home and going to the movie theater.

Video at Home	Movie Theater

Activity 2

Comprehension

Discuss the two activities. Tell about a time you went to the movies and a time you watched a video at home. What was the most fun about each?

_____

_____

_____

_____

_____

_____

_____

_____

Application

Your group will act out having a good time at the movies or having a good time watching a video at home. Try to think of all the fun things that might happen before, during, and after the show.

_____
_____
_____
_____
_____
_____
_____
_____

Analysis

Compare the two activities. How are they alike and how are they different?

Alike	Different

Synthesis

You will get a piece of drawing paper for this activity. Draw a movie poster advertising your favorite movie, or design a video sleeve for it. Include information about the stars and why it is a good movie.

Evaluation

Write the pluses and minuses about watching a video and going to the movies.

Pluses About a Video	Minuses About a Video

Pluses About the Movie Theater	Minuses About the Movie Theater

© 1996 Good Apple

Home Video or Movie Theater?

I think _____ is more fun than _____

Three reasons I think this are _____

_____

• One reason I think this is _____

_____

I know this because _____

_____

• The second reason I think this is _____

_____

This is true because _____

_____

• The last reason I think this is _____

_____

I know this because _____

_____

I think we should _____

instead of _____

because _____

_____

_____

_____

_____

Name _____

Seeing a Video at Home or Going to the Movie Theater?

Paragraph 1: Introduction and three reasons that support my position

I think _____ would be more fun than _____

The first reason I think this is _____

_____

The second reason is _____

_____

The third reason is _____

_____

Paragraph 2: Reason 1 supported

Reason 1 restated: _____

_____

Support idea 1: _____

_____

Support idea 2: _____

_____

Support idea 3: _____

_____

Paragraph 3: Reason 2 supported

Reason 2 restated: _____

_____

Support idea 1: _____

_____

Support idea 2: _____

_____

Support idea 3: _____

_____

Paragraph 4: Reason 3 supported

Reason 3 restated: _____

_____

Support idea 1: _____

_____

Support idea 2: _____

_____

Support idea 3: _____

_____

Paragraph 5: Summary

Restate position with most important point. _____

_____

Make a statement or two regarding the importance of your position. _____

_____

_____

_____

A Class Without Rules?

Introduction

The object of this lesson is for students to use a variety of thinking skills to make and support a decision about rules. The activity concludes with students writing a persuasive essay to support their decision.

This Sequential Thinking Lesson can be done with all grade levels. It uses class rules, well known to all students, as concrete concepts that enable students to generate and process a great deal of information. Part I of the lesson uses the taxonomy to gather and process information. It is designed to be done in cooperative groups or as a whole class. Each activity has student recording guides following the teacher directions. Part II of the lesson has students use one of three writing templates to generate a persuasive position paper. Directions for using the templates begin on page 25. Part II should be completed individually.

- Estimated time: 3 to 5 hours over 3 to 5 days

- Curriculum knowledge needed by students: None

Role of the Teacher

The role of the teacher in this and all Sequential Lessons is that of a facilitator. If students have practiced the thinking taxonomy and are comfortable with the levels of the taxonomy, Part I will be simple. If they have not done much work with the thinking taxonomy, the teacher will have to provide more direction. Part I has six activities. The teacher should introduce each activity. After introducing the activity, give one or two examples to get the groups started. Once groups have started, move from group to group encouraging expansive and creative thought.

PART I: Information Gathering and Processing

Introduce the lesson by asking, "Which is better for learning, a class with rules or one without rules?" At this point, most students will have an opinion—but they will not be able to defend their positions or convince others that their choice is the best. The purpose of the next few activities is to gather enough information to support their opinions in a way that will persuade others to think as they do.

Each group should have a copy of the recording guides to complete as they go through each activity.

Activity 1 Knowledge and Comprehension

Each group will discuss classroom rules that they have had to follow since they have been in school. After doing this, have students record four of the rules and list their understanding of the purpose of each rule.

Activity 1 *(Example)*

Rule	Purpose of the Rule
Raise your hand to talk.	So we can hear who is talking
Stay in your seat.	To keep us from bothering each other

Activity 2 Application

Each group will discuss the purpose of rules and other places besides school that have rules. Have students list three places other than school that have rules and list one rule from each place as an example of its rules.

Activity 3 Analysis

Have each group analyze the unwritten rules of the classroom. Have students list all the rules that they follow that aren't written down as class rules. Have them state why these rules are important.

Activity 3 *(Example)*

Unwritten Rule	Why It Is Important
No spitting on the floor	It's gross and spreads germs.
No laughing at others	It makes people feel bad.
No cheating	It's not fair.

Activity 4 Synthesis

Have each group formulate four rules that would make the class or school better. Students should state their reason for each rule. After they do this, have them formulate a list of consequences for breaking these rules.

Activity 5 Evaluation

Have each group complete the pluses-and-minuses chart. Make sure that students refer to the information gathered in the first five activities.

Activity 5 *(Example)*

Pluses of Rules	Minuses of Rules
They keep the room quiet.	Sometimes class gets boring.
They keep you safe.	You get into trouble.
They make it peaceful.	I like to talk when I work.

PART II: Writing the Persuasive Paper

NOTE: Directions for writing the persuasive paper and using the writing templates begin on page 25.

Knowledge and Comprehension

Think about all the rules you have had to follow since you have been in school. What are they, and what is the purpose of each rule?

Rule	Purpose of the Rule

Application

Think about other places besides school that have rules. List three other places and give an example of a rule from each.

Place	Sample Rule
1.	
2.	
3.	

Analysis

There are many unwritten rules at school. For instance, you can't climb the fence and go home. Think of several unwritten school and class rules. What are they, and why are they important?

Unwritten Rule	Importance

Synthesis

Your group needs to think up four rules to make your school or classroom better. State each rule and then give a reason for the rule. After that, make up four consequences for breaking the rules.

Rules	Consequences

Rule 1: _____ First Consequence: _____

Reason: _____ _____

Rule 2: _____ Second Consequence: _____

Reason: _____ _____

Rule 3: _____ Third Consequence: _____

Reason: _____ _____

Rule 4: _____ Fourth Consequence: _____

Reason: _____ _____

Evaluation

Write the pluses and minuses of rules.

Pluses About Rules	Minuses About Rules

 © 1996 Good Apple

A Class Without Rules?

I think a class _____ (with/without) rules is better than

a class _____ (with/without) rules.

Three reasons I think this are _____

_____

_____

• One reason I think this is _____

_____

I know this because _____

_____

• The second reason I think this is _____

_____

This is true because _____

_____

• The last reason I think this is _____

_____

I know this because _____

_____

I think we should _____ rules because _____

_____

_____

_____

_____

Name

A Class Without Rules?

Paragraph 1: Introduction and three reasons that support my position.

I think a class _____ (with/without) rules is better

than a class _____ (with/without) rules.

The first reason I think this is _____

_____

The second reason is _____

_____

The third reason is _____

_____

Paragraph 2: Reason 1 supported

Reason 1 restated: _____

_____

Support idea 1: _____

_____

Support idea 2: _____

_____

Support idea 3: _____

_____

Paragraph 3: Reason 2 supported

Reason 2 restated: _____

_____

Support idea 1: _____

_____

Support idea 2: _____

_____

Support idea 3: _____

_____

Paragraph 4: Reason 3 supported

Reason 3 restated: _____

_____

Support idea 1: _____

_____

Support idea 2: _____

_____

Support idea 3: _____

_____

Paragraph 5: Summary

Restate position with most important point. _____

_____

Make a statement or two regarding the importance of your position. _____

_____

_____

_____

_____

City Life or Country Life?

Introduction

The object of this lesson is for students to use a variety of thinking skills to make and support a decision about where they would like to live. The lesson concludes with students writing a persuasive essay to support their decision.

This Sequential Thinking Lesson can be done with all grade levels. It is a particularly good lesson to be done at the conclusion of a unit about city and country life. Part I of the lesson uses the taxonomy to gather and process information. It is designed to be done in cooperative groups or as a whole class. Each activity has student recording guides following the teacher directions. Part II of the lesson has students use one of three writing templates to generate a persuasive position paper. Directions for using the templates begin on page 25. Part II should be completed individually.

- Estimated time: 3 to 5 hours over 3 to 5 days

- Curriculum knowledge needed by students: None

Role of the Teacher

The role of the teacher in this and all Sequential Lessons is that of a facilitator. If students have practiced the thinking taxonomy and are comfortable with the levels of the taxonomy, Part I will be simple. If they have not done much work with the thinking taxonomy, the teacher will have to provide more direction. The teacher should introduce each activity. After introducing the activity, give one or two examples to get the groups started. Once groups are started, move from group to group, encouraging expansive and creative thought.

PART I: Information Gathering and Processing

Introduce the lesson by asking the question, "Which is better, living in the city or living in the country?" At this point, most students will have an opinion—but they will not be able to defend their positions or convince others that their choice is the best. The purpose of the next few activities is to gather enough information to support their opinions in a way that will persuade others to think as they do.

If the lesson is being done in groups, each group should have a copy of the recording guides to complete as they go through each activity. If the lesson is being done as a whole class, the teacher can do all the recording, or students can copy the teacher recording.

Activity 1 Knowledge

Groups generate a list of facts about each place.

Activity 1 *(Example)*

City Life	Country Life
Entertainment	Fishing
Lots of people	Few people
Buses	No malls

Activity 2 Comprehension

To demonstrate a better understanding of the attributes of a good place to live, have each group compile a list of attributes needed to make a place livable.

Activity 2 *(Example)*

- Lots of water
- Entertainment
- Parks
- Fresh, clean air
- A place to get food
- A way to get to places

Activity 3 Application

Have each group make two posters or murals illustrating a view of the country and of the city. Make sure students include some of the attributes that they have included in Activity 2.

Activity 4 Analysis

Have each group compare the two locations. How are they alike and how are they different?

Activity 4 *(Example)*

How are they alike?	How are they different?
Both have water.	The city has traffic.
Both have places to live.	The country has more trees.
Both have shopping.	The city has more movies.

Activity 5 Synthesis

In this activity, students create the perfect town and then draw a travel poster that will persuade people to move to their town. The town can include anything students want. It can have country or city attributes or a combination of both. Groups should be encouraged to be creative and invent a "new and improved" community to live in. It is a good idea to share a travel brochure or some vacation advertisements from magazines to give groups ideas for their posters.

Activity 6 Evaluation

Have each group complete the pluses-and-minuses chart. Make sure that students refer to the information gathered in the first five activities.

Activity 6 *(Example)*

Pluses of the City	Minuses of the City
Entertainment	Crowded
Lots of people	Lots of crime
Lots of jobs	No place to play

PART II: Writing the Persuasive Paper

NOTE: Directions for writing the persuasive paper and using the writing templates begin on page 25.

Knowledge

Write as many facts about the city and the country as your group can think of.

City	Country

Activity 2

Comprehension

Discuss the two places to live. What are attributes (requirements)
of a good place to live?

_____

_____

_____

_____

_____

_____

_____

_____

_____

© 1996 Good Apple

Application

Make two posters or murals, one illustrating a view of the country, and one illustrating a view of the city. Make sure each poster includes some of the attributes you included in Activity 2.

Analysis

Compare the two places. How are they alike and how are they different?

Alike	Different

   © 1996 Good Apple

Synthesis

Discuss in your group what the ideal place to live would be like. Now draw an advertising poster to persuade people to move to your "new and improved" community. Be creative.

© 1996 Good Apple

Evaluation

Write the pluses and minuses about the city and the country.

Pluses About the City	Minuses About the City

Pluses About the Country	Minuses About the Country

City Life or Country Life?

I think living in the _____ is better than living in the _____

Three reasons I think this are _____

_____

_____

• One reason I think this is _____

_____

I know this because _____

_____

• The second reason I think this is _____

_____

This is true because _____

_____

• The last reason I think this is _____

_____

I know this because _____

_____

I think living in the _____ is better than living in the _____

because _____

_____

_____

_____

City Life or Country Life?

Paragraph 1: Introduction and three reasons that support my position

I think living in the _____ would be better than living in the _____

The first reason I think this is _____

_____

The second reason is _____

_____

The third reason is _____

_____

Paragraph 2: Reason 1 supported

Reason 1 restated: _____

_____

Support idea 1: _____

_____

Support idea 2: _____

_____

Support idea 3: _____

_____

Paragraph 3: Reason 2 supported

Reason 2 restated: _____

_____

Support idea 1: _____

_____

Support idea 2: _____

_____

Support idea 3: _____

_____

Paragraph 4: Reason 3 supported

Reason 3 restated: _____

_____

Support idea 1: _____

_____

Support idea 2: _____

_____

Support idea 3: _____

_____

Paragraph 5: Summary

Restate position with most important point. _____

_____

Make a statement or two regarding the importance of your position.

_____

_____

_____

_____

Picking a President

Introduction

The object of this lesson is for students to use a variety of thinking skills to make and support a decision about voting for a president. The lesson concludes with students writing a persuasive essay to support their decision.

This Sequential Thinking Lesson can be done with intermediate and upper-grade students. It is a particularly good lesson to be done in correlation with a unit about presidents, democracy, or during an election year. Part I of the lesson uses the taxonomy to gather and process information. It is designed to be done in cooperative groups or as a whole class. Each activity has student recording guides following the teacher directions. Part II of the lesson has students use one of three writing templates to generate a persuasive position paper. Directions for using the templates begin on page 25. Part II should be completed individually.

- Estimated time: 3 to 5 hours over 3 to 5 days

- Curriculum knowledge needed by the student: Knowledge of the election and campaign process as well as an understanding of propaganda is helpful.

Role of the Teacher

The role of the teacher in this and all Sequential Lessons is that of a facilitator. If students have practiced the thinking taxonomy and are comfortable with the levels of the taxonomy, Part I will be simple. If they have not done much work with the thinking taxonomy, the teacher will have to provide more direction. The teacher should introduce each activity. After introducing the activity, give one or two examples to get the groups started. Once groups are started, move from group to group, encouraging expansive and creative thought.

PART I: Information Gathering and Processing

Introduce the lesson by discussing elections, campaign strategies, and propaganda. Make sure that students understand that a candidate's goal in an election is to win and that there is often a motive behind promises. After the discussion, go on to Activity 1. At this point, most students will have an opinion—but they will not be able to defend their positions or convince others that their choice is the best. The purpose of the next few activities is to gather enough information to support their opinions in a way that will persuade others to think as they do. If you need help with the lesson design, see the directions for the "Dog Dilemma or Cat Taskgraphy?" lesson.

If the lesson is being done in groups, each group should have a copy of the recording guides to complete as they go through each activity. If the lesson is being done as a whole class, the teacher can do all the recording, or students can copy the teacher recording.

Activity 1   Knowledge and Comprehension

Pass out the candidate-information sheets. Let groups review the information about each candidate. Without forming an opinion, have each group write a paragraph about each candidate.

Activity 1 *(Example)*

Bobby is a boy in the fifth grade. This is his first year at this school. He likes track and going to the zoo. His favorite subject is reading. He likes ice cream and pizza. He is in favor of field trips, assemblies, nutrition break, computers, and TV. He would make the school day shorter by increasing homework.

Activity 2   Application and Synthesis

This activity combines the application and synthesis activities. Each group writes a 100-150 word campaign speech for each candidate. Have groups share their speeches with the rest of the class.

Have each group make a campaign poster for each candidate. If you are doing this activity during an election year, there will be many posters to bring in as examples.

At the conclusion of the lesson, have a secret-ballot election to see which candidate wins.

Activity 3   Analysis

Have each group compare the two candidates. How are they alike and how are they different?

Activity 3 *(Example)*

How are they alike?	How are they different?
Both in fifth grade	Boy vs. girl
Both favor nutrition break	Like different foods
Both want computers	Different goals

Activity 4   Evaluation

When voting for a candidate, it is important to vote for a candidate who thinks about issues in the same way you do. The common-issue charts enable students to compare themselves to the candidates. This chart is similar to the pluses-and-minuses chart in other lessons. It is probably a good idea to have each student do an individual common-interests chart, since groups would have difficulty agreeing on common interests.

Interests I Have in Common with Bobby	Differences I Have with Bobby
Good at track	I don't want more homework.
Like pizza	I don't like field trips.
Want library open at night	I don't like reading.

PART II: Writing the Persuasive Paper

NOTE: Directions for writing the persuasive paper and using the writing templates begin on page 25.

All About Suzie

FACT SHEET

My name is Suzie. My main goal as president is to eliminate homework by making our school day 30 minutes longer.

- I'm in fifth grade, and have gone to this school for five years.
- My favorite subjects are math and science.
- I love sports. I am captain of my soccer team. I want an after-school sports program. My dad is a high-school coach.
- My favorite food is tacos. I am in favor of having a nutrition break every day.
- All classes should have computers and a TV.
- I think every class should go on field trips.
- We should have one assembly every month.
- School should be open Saturdays for sports teams.
- When I grow up, I am going to be a doctor.
- I get A's and B's on my report card.
- I think video games at school are stupid.

She Likes	**She Dislikes**
• Running	• Gossip
• Recess and lunch	• Cheaters
• Music and TV	• Rainy days
• Tacos	• Peas
• Blue	• Pink
• Mountain bikes	• Tattletales
• Going to the park	• Being grounded
• The beach	• Camping

© 1996 Good Apple

All About Bobby

FACT SHEET

My name is Bobby. My main goal as president is to shorten the school day by increasing homework 30 minutes each day.

- I'm in fifth grade, and have gone to this school for one year.
- My favorite subject is reading.
- I love sports. I am captain of my track team.
- My favorite foods are pizza and ice cream. I am in favor of having a nutrition break every day.
- All classes should have computers and a TV.
- I think every class should go on field trips.
- We should have one assembly every month.
- We should have a video-game room for play during recess.
- When I grow up, I am going to be a teacher.
- I get A's and B's on my report card.
- The library should be open at night for studying and homework.

He Likes	He Dislikes
• Reading books	• Liars
• Recess and lunch	• Making fun of people
• Going to the movies	• Braggarts
• Pizza	• Corn
• Blue	• Orange
• Kites	• Baby sitters
• Going to the zoo	• Being grounded

Knowledge and Comprehension

Review the fact sheets about Bobby and Suzie. Without forming an opinion, write a paragraph about each candidate. Tell about their likes, their goals, and what they support.

About Bobby: _____

_____

_____

_____

_____

_____

_____

_____

About Suzie: _____

_____

_____

_____

_____

_____

_____

_____

_____

© 1996 Good Apple

Application and Synthesis

Write a 100-150 word campaign speech for each candidate. Then share your speeches with the rest of the class.

Suzie's Speech: _____

_____

_____

_____

_____

_____

_____

Bobby's Speech: _____

_____

_____

_____

_____

_____

_____

Now make a campaign poster for each candidate.

Analysis

Compare the two candidates. How are they alike and how are they different?

Alike	Different

© 1996 Good Apple

Evaluation

Write common interests and differences you have with each candidate.

Things I Have in Common with Bobby	Differences I Have with Bobby

Things I Have in Common with Suzie	Differences I Have with Suzie

© 1996 Good Apple

Picking a President

I think _____ would be a better president than _____

Three reasons I think this are _____

_____

• One reason I think this is _____

_____

I know this because _____

_____

• The second reason I think this is _____

_____

This is true because _____

_____

• The last reason I think this is _____

_____

I know this because _____

_____

I think you should vote for _____ instead of _____

because _____

_____

_____

_____

_____

Picking a President

Paragraph 1: Introduction and three reasons that support my position

I think _____ would be a better president than _____

The first reason I think this is _____

_____

The second reason is _____

_____

The third reason is _____

_____

Paragraph 2: Reason 1 supported

Reason 1 restated: _____

_____

Support idea 1: _____

_____

Support idea 2: _____

_____

Support idea 3: _____

_____

Paragraph 3: Reason 2 supported

Reason 2 restated: _____

_____

Support idea 1: _____

_____

Support idea 2: _____

_____

Support idea 3: _____

_____

Paragraph 4: Reason 3 supported

Reason 3 restated: _____

_____

Support idea 1: _____

_____

Support idea 2: _____

_____

Support idea 3: _____

_____

Paragraph 5: Summary

Restate position with most important point. _____

_____

_____

Make a statement or two regarding the importance of your position.

_____

_____

_____

_____

President or King,
Democracy or Monarchy?

Introduction

The object of this lesson is for students to use a variety of thinking skills to make and support a decision about governments. The lesson concludes with students writing a persuasive essay to support their decision.

This Sequential Thinking Lesson can be done with intermediate and upper-grade students. It can also be done as an oral activity with primary students. It is a particularly good lesson to be done in correlation with a unit on colonization and the Revolutionary War. Primary students enjoy doing the lesson after a unit on fairy tales and often have different perspectives than older students. Part I of the lesson uses the taxonomy to gather and process information. It is designed to be done in cooperative groups or as a whole class. Each activity has student recording guides following the teacher directions. Part II of the lesson has students use one of three writing templates to generate a persuasive position paper. Directions for using the templates begin on page 25. Part II should be completed individually.

- Estimated time: 3 to 5 hours over 3 to 5 days

- Curriculum knowledge needed by students: Knowledge of monarchy, democracy, presidents, and kings is helpful.

Role of the Teacher

The role of the teacher in this and all Sequential Lessons is that of a facilitator. If students have practiced the thinking taxonomy and are comfortable with the levels of the taxonomy, Part I will be simple. If they have not done much work with the thinking taxonomy, the teacher will have to provide more direction. The teacher should introduce each activity. After introducing the activity, give one or two examples to get the groups started. Once groups are started, move from group to group, encouraging expansive and creative thought.

PART I: Information Gathering and Processing

Introduce the lesson by asking, "Which is better, living in a democracy and having a president or living in a monarchy and having a king?" At this point, most students will have an opinion—but they will not be able to defend their positions or convince others that their choice is the best. The purpose of the next few activities is to gather enough information to support their opinions in a way that will persuade others to think as they do. If you need help with the lesson design, see the directions for the "Dog Dilemma or Cat Taskgraphy?" lesson.

If the lesson is being done in groups, each group should have a copy of the recording guides to complete as they go through each activity. If the lesson is being done as a whole class, the teacher can do all the recording, or students can copy the teacher's recording.

Activity 1 Knowledge

Have the groups list facts about each form of government.

Activity 1 *(Example)*

Democracy	Monarchy
Elections	Kings and queens
Possible corruption	Loyalty
Vote on laws	Servants

Activity 2 Comprehension

To demonstrate a better understanding of living in a democracy and in a monarchy, have students discuss and write a paragraph about what it would be like to live under each form of government.

Activity 3 Application

Have a class election. You can vote for officers, for a new class rule, for a class reward, for monitors, and so on. It is important to let students participate in some kind of campaign for office, or in support of an issue.

After a day of elections, the teacher can play king or queen for a day. Choose class officers and make up unfair rules. Give the class an opportunity to see both sides of each system in practice.

Activity 4   Analysis

Have each group compare the forms of government. How are they alike and how are they different?

Activity 4 *(Example)*

How are they alike?	How are they different?
Both have laws.	Democracy has elections.
Both have taxes.	People can get rid of bad elected officials.
Both have public services.	

Activity 5   Synthesis

Have students answer this question: Would you rather be a king/queen or a president? Then have students give 5 reasons to support their choices. You probably want to have students answer the question individually.

Activity 6   Evaluation

Have each group complete the pluses-and-minuses chart. Make sure that students refer to the information gathered in the first five activities.

Activity 6 *(Example)*

Pluses of a Monarchy	Minuses of a Monarchy
No corrupt elections	No voice in government
Kings don't have to play politics to get elected.	Can't get rid of bad ruler
	Can't become ruler unless born into royal family

PART II: Writing the Persuasive Paper

NOTE: *Directions for writing the persuasive paper and using the writing templates begin on page 25.*

President or King?

Knowledge

Write as many facts about a monarchy and a democracy as you can.

Monarchy	Democracy

Comprehension

Discuss the two forms of government. Write a paragraph about each.

Monarchy: _____

_____

_____

_____

Democracy: _____

_____

_____

_____

Now hold a class election. Your teacher will guide you.

Analysis

Compare the forms of government. How are they alike? How are they different?

Synthesis

Discuss in your group what it would be like to be king/queen or president. Which would you rather be? Give 5 reasons to support your choice.

I would rather be a _____

Reason 1: _____

_____

Reason 2: _____

_____

Reason 3: _____

_____

Reason 4: _____

_____

Reason 5: _____

_____

Evaluation

Write the pluses and minuses about monarchy and democracy.

Pluses About Monarchy	Minuses About Monarchy

Pluses About Democracy	Minuses About Democracy

© 1996 Good Apple   *Activity 6*

Name _____

President or King?

I think having a _____ is better than having a _____

Three reasons I think this are _____

_____

• One reason I think this is _____

_____

I know this because _____

_____

• The second reason I think this is _____

_____

This is true because _____

_____

• The last reason I think this is _____

_____

I know this because _____

_____

I think we should have a _____ instead of a _____

because _____

_____

_____

_____

_____

_____

President or King, Democracy or Monarchy?

Paragraph 1: Introduction and three reasons that support my position

I think having a _____ would be better than having a _____

The first reason I think this is _____

_____

The second reason is _____

_____

The third reason is _____

_____

Paragraph 2: Reason 1 supported

Reason 1 restated: _____

_____

Support idea 1: _____

_____

Support idea 2: _____

_____

Support idea 3: _____

_____

Paragraph 3: Reason 2 supported

Reason 2 restated: _____

_____

Support idea 1: _____

_____

Support idea 2: _____

_____

Support idea 3: _____

_____

Paragraph 4: Reason 3 supported

Reason 3 restated: _____

_____

Support idea 1: _____

_____

Support idea 2: _____

_____

Support idea 3: _____

_____

Paragraph 5: Summary

Restate position with most important point. _____

_____

Make a statement or two regarding the importance of your position.

_____

_____

_____

_____

Save the Rain Forests?

Introduction

The object of this lesson is for students to use a variety of thinking skills to make and support a decision about saving the rain forests. The lesson concludes with students writing a persuasive essay to support their decision.

This Sequential Thinking Lesson can be done by intermediate and upper-grade students. It also makes a good oral lesson for primary students because of their interest in the rain forests. It is a high-interest lesson about a controversial topic. This lesson can be done in correlation with a science unit on ecology or endangered species, or in conjunction with Earth Day. There are many trade books, videos, and other materials that provide excellent background information for study before the lesson begins. Most students, by nature, will favor the conservation of rain forests because of their love for animals and nature. Be sure that, at the end of the lesson, they understand that there are two sides to the issue and that there are many valid reasons for the development of rain forest lands. Included are information sheets highlighting both sides of the issue.

Part I of the lesson uses the taxonomy to gather and process information. Part II of the lesson has students use one of three writing templates to generate a persuasive position paper. Directions for using the templates begin on page 25.

- Estimated time: 4 to 6 hours over 4 to 6 days

- Curriculum knowledge needed by students: Knowledge of ecology, endangered species, and of the needs of third-world countries is helpful.

Role of the Teacher

The role of the teacher in this and all Sequential Lessons is that of a facilitator. After introducing the activity, give one or two examples to get the groups started. Once groups are started, move from group to group, encouraging expansive and creative thought.

PART I: Information Gathering and Processing

Introduce the lesson by discussing or reviewing information presented in the information sheet, along with any other information that might have been studied previously. If this lesson is done at the conclusion of a unit, a quick unit review is helpful. Ask students, "Should we continue to cut down our rain forests?" After a brief discussion, in which students share "impulsive" opinions, go on with the lesson.

If the lesson is being done in groups, each group should have a copy of the recording guides to complete as they go through each activity. If the lesson is being done as a whole class, the teacher can do all the recording, or students can copy the teacher's recording.

Activity 1   Knowledge

Pass out the information sheets for group review. After review of this and other information, have each group list the facts they know about rain forests. They can use the information on the information sheets and additional information available from a unit of study, an encyclopedia, or trade books.

Activity 2   Comprehension

Without forming an opinion, have each group write a paragraph summarizing the important points of each side of the issue.

Activity 2 *(Example)*

People are starving all over the world. Development of the rain forests is the only way that these people can be fed and their countries can be developed. Farming rain forests provides crops and grazing land for cattle. In addition, many medicines and other useful products are made from natural resources found in the rain forests. Gold, oil, other minerals, and lumber are also plentiful in the rain forests. Efforts are being made to care for and replant the rain forests.

Activity 3 Analysis

Have each group discuss the resources of the rain forests that are useful to us. Have students make a ranked list, with the resource they think is most important first.

Activity 3 *(Example)*

1. *Chemicals for medicines*
2. *Farming*
3. *Raising cattle*

Activity 4 Application and Synthesis

Have students draw and label a section of the rain forest and tell how the objects in their pictures rely on each other for food, protection, shelter, and so on.

Activity 5 Evaluation

Have each group complete the pluses-and-minuses chart about conserving our rain forests.

Activity 5 *(Example)*

Pluses of Conserving Our Rain Forests	Minuses of Conserving Our Rain Forests
Protects endangered species	Resources needed for medicine
Oxygen	Needed farmlands
Erosion protection	Needed lumber

PART II: Writing the Persuasive Paper

NOTE: Directions for writing the persuasive paper and using the writing templates begin on page 25.

Save the Rain Forests

FACT SHEET

Every minute, 50 acres of rain forests are cut down!

- Rain forests are home to millions of species of plants, animals, and insects. Cutting down rain forests destroys the habitat of these species.

- Slash-and-burn farmers destroy habitats for farmlands. Burning trees causes air pollution and destroys oxygen-producing trees.

- In the poorest countries, people are forced to destroy or sell their lands in order to have food. Rich countries must help poor countries without harming our environment.

- One-fourth of all our medicine comes from rain forests. If we lose the rain forests, we lose our sources for these medicines.

- More than half of the world's rain forests have been destroyed in the last 50 years. At this rate, there will be no rain forests by the year 2050.

© 1996 Good Apple

Use the Rain Forests

FACT SHEET

We rely on the lands occupied by rain forests to produce food for the millions of people in our world who are starving.

- Nearly 40,000 children in the world die from starvation and disease each day. The fertile grounds of the rain forests are desperately needed to produce food to defeat world hunger.

- Industrial foresters and miners provide great economic opportunities to the poor and underdeveloped rain-forest countries.

- Rain forests provide resources, which are used to produce medicines and other products.

- Rain forest lands provide excellent grazing fields for livestock, which produce much of the meat consumed in the world today.

What Comes From the Rain Forest?

- Lumber
- Wool for sweaters
- Chemicals for cosmetics
- Fruits, vegetables, nuts
- 25% of all medicines
- Alternate forms of fuel
- Safe pesticides
- Hardwoods for furniture
- Rubber
- Cocoa and coffee
- Farmlands and food
- Copper, iron, uranium

Knowledge

Write as many facts as you can about rain forests.

_____

_____

_____

_____

_____

_____

_____

Activity 2

Comprehension

Without forming an opinion, write a paragraph summarizing the important points of each side of the issue.

Save the Rain Forests: _____

_____

_____

_____

_____

_____

Use the Rain Forests: _____

_____

_____

_____

_____

_____

Analysis

Brainstorm a list of ways rain forests are useful. Rank them according to which uses you think are the most important.

1. _____   11. _____
2. _____   12. _____
3. _____   13. _____
4. _____   14. _____
5. _____   15. _____
6. _____   16. _____
7. _____   17. _____
8. _____   18. _____
9. _____   19. _____
10. _____   20. _____

Application and Synthesis

Draw and label a section of the rain forest. Tell how the objects in your picture rely on each other for food, protection, shelter and so on. Write your notes below. Then use a separate paper for your picture.

_____

_____

_____

_____

_____

_____

Evaluation

Write the pluses and minuses, as you see them, about conserving our rain forests.

Pluses of Conserving the Rain Forests	Minuses of Conserving the Rain Forests

 © 1996 Good Apple

Save the Rain Forests?

I am _____ (*in favor of/opposed to*) saving the rain forests.

Three reasons are _____

_____

• One reason I think this is _____

_____

I know this because _____

_____

• The second reason I think this is _____

_____

This is true because _____

_____

• The last reason I think this is _____

_____

I know this because _____

_____

I think the rain forests _____ (*should/should not*) be saved

because _____

_____

_____

_____

_____

Name

Save the Rain Forests?

Paragraph 1: Introduction and three reasons that support my position

I _____ (*support/oppose*) saving the rain forests.

The first reason is _____

_____

The second reason is _____

_____

The third reason is _____

_____

Paragraph 2: Reason 1 supported

Reason 1 restated: _____

_____

Support idea 1: _____

_____

Support idea 2: _____

_____

Support idea 3: _____

_____

Paragraph 3: Reason 2 supported

Reason 2 restated: _____

_____

Support idea 1: _____

_____

Support idea 2: _____

_____

Support idea 3: _____

_____

Paragraph 4: Reason 3 supported

Reason 3 restated: _____

_____

Support idea 1: _____

_____

Support idea 2: _____

_____

Support idea 3: _____

_____

Paragraph 5: Summary

Restate position with most important point. _____

_____

_____

Make a statement or two regarding the importance of your position. _____

_____

_____

_____

_____

Nuclear Energy: Pro or Con?

Introduction

The object of this lesson is for students to use a variety of thinking skills to make and support decisions about nuclear energy. The lesson concludes with students writing a persuasive essay to support their decision.

This Sequential Thinking Lesson is at the upper-elementary and middle-school level. It is an example of a content lesson, and should be used after a unit on energy or pollution. It provides a good way to find out what students learned in an authentic manner, as opposed to a typical unit test. It also is a good lesson to use as a model for teacher-developed lessons that would serve to summarize and assess student learning at the completion of a science or social studies unit in which the issues were examined.

Part I of the lesson uses the taxonomy to gather and process information. Part II of the lesson has students use one of three writing templates to generate a persuasive position paper. Directions for using the templates begin on page 25. The lesson should be done over four to six language arts or science periods, depending on the level of the students.

- Estimated time: 4 to 6 hours over 4 to 6 days

- Curriculum knowledge needed by students: Knowledge of energy forms, nuclear energy, ecology, and pollution is helpful.

Role of the Teacher

The role of the teacher in this and all Sequential Lessons is that of a facilitator. After introducing the activity, give one or two examples to get the groups started. Once groups are started, move from group to group encouraging expansive and creative thought.

PART I: Information Gathering and Processing

Introduce the lesson by discussing or reviewing information about different energy forms. If this lesson is done at the conclusion of a unit, a quick unit review is helpful. This lesson includes pro-and-con nuclear energy fact sheets that can also be used to review information regarding nuclear energy. Ask students, "Should we continue to build nuclear power plants?" After a brief discussion in which students share "impulsive" opinions, proceed with the lesson.

If the lesson is being done in groups, each group should have a copy of the recording guides to complete as they go through each activity. If the lesson is being done as a whole class, the teacher can do all the recording, or students can copy the teacher's recording.

Activity 1 Knowledge

Pass out the Nuclear Energy Fact Sheets. Let groups review the pro-and-con information. Have each group list the facts they know about nuclear energy. They can use the information on the sheets, plus any additional information available from a unit of study, an encyclopedia, or trade books.

Activity 2 Comprehension

Without forming an opinion, have each group write a paragraph summarizing the important points of each side of the issue.

Activity 2 (Example)

Nuclear energy is a limitless form of power. Unlike other forms of energy, there is no pollution to the environment during the energy-generating process. Nuclear waste can be stored safely so that it never presents a problem to our environment or health. Nuclear energy has become an important tool used by doctors. The limitless power source of nuclear energy has made deep-space travel a reality.

Activity 3 Analysis

Have each group compare nuclear energy and another energy source, such as water, oil, solar panels, or coal.

Activity 3 *(Example)*
Comparing Nuclear Energy to Oil Energy

How are they alike?	How are they different?
Both produce heat.	Oil provides a more portable energy source.
Both produce electricity.	
Both produce jobs.	Oil is running out.

Activity 4 Application and Synthesis

Select one of these options:

- Ask students to discuss how they would feel if a group wanted to build a nuclear power plant in their community. Have each group of students make campaign posters favoring the plant *and* opposing the plant.

- Have each group draw and label a house having a portable nuclear reactor, which provides power for the entire house. Be sure that students draw and label special safety features of the reactor and of the house.

- Have students brainstorm a list of alternate energy sources and how they could be used to replace nuclear energy.

Activity 5 Evaluation

Have each group complete the pluses-and-minuses chart about nuclear energy.

Activity 5 *(Example)*

Pluses of Nuclear Energy	Minuses of Nuclear Energy
Limitless	Waste disposal
No air pollution	Accident potential
Medical uses	Faulty equipment

PART II: Writing the Persuasive Paper

NOTE: *Directions for writing the persuasive paper and using the writing templates begin on page 25.*

Support Nuclear Energy

FACT SHEET

Nuclear energy is the energy source of the future!

- Nuclear energy is limitless. We don't have to rely on other countries for fuel.

- Oil, coal, and natural gas supplies are dwindling.

- 22% of our nation's energy comes from nuclear power plants.

- One-third of all hospital patients are treated with nuclear medicine.

Benefits

- Nuclear-powered submarines

- Deep-space travel

- Cancer and heart treatments

- High safety regulations assure safety.

- Oil used to make electricity and power cars is a major contributor to air pollution.

- Nuclear-generated electricity is much cheaper than oil-fired electricity.

- Proper disposal of waste guarantees safety.

- Nuclear power plants produce thousands of jobs.

© 1996 Good Apple

Oppose Nuclear Energy

FACT SHEET

Nuclear energy is a disaster waiting to happen. Besides, where do we bury the waste?

- Radioactive waste has cost billions of dollars to clean up.
- A simple stuck valve could cause a disaster that would contaminate a whole city and kill thousands, as it almost did at Three Mile Island, in 1979.
- In 1986 there was a meltdown in Russia at Chernobyl. Radiation leaks caused hundreds of deaths.
- Old plants will begin to crack and release deadly radioactivity.

Nuclear Energy is a Threat to all People

- Malfunctioning equipment or human error could cause a disaster at any moment.
- Nuclear waste could remain radioactive for millions of years.

Alternate Energy Sources and Solutions

- Energy-efficient appliances
- Public transportation
- Carpooling
- Wind
- Water
- Solar
- Coal
- Oil

© 1996 Good Apple

Knowledge

Review the information you have on nuclear energy. Write as many
facts as you can.

_____

_____

_____

_____

_____

_____

Activity 2

Comprehension

Without forming an opinion, write a paragraph summarizing the
important points of each side of the issue.

Favoring Nuclear Energy _____

_____

_____

_____

_____

Opposing Nuclear Energy _____

_____

_____

_____

_____

Analysis

Compare nuclear energy with another energy form.

Nuclear Energy Compared with _____

Alike	Different

Application and Synthesis

You have three choices of activities to do with your group. Your teacher has the directions. Write your notes below.

_____

_____

_____

_____

_____

_____

Evaluation

Write the pluses and minuses about nuclear energy.

Pluses of Nuclear Energy	Minuses of Nuclear Energy

 © 1996 Good Apple

Name

Nuclear Energy: Pro or Con?

I am _____ (*in favor of/opposed to*) nuclear energy.

Three reasons are _____

_____

• One reason I think this is _____

_____

I know this because _____

_____

• The second reason I think this is _____

_____

This is true because _____

_____

• The last reason I think this is _____

_____

I know this because _____

_____

I think we _____ (*should/should not*) use nuclear energy
because _____

_____

_____

_____

Nuclear Energy: Pro or Con?

Paragraph 1: Introduction and three reasons that support my position

I _____ (*support* or *oppose*) nuclear energy.

The first reason is _____

_____

The second reason is _____

_____

The third reason is _____

_____

Paragraph 2: Reason 1 supported

Reason 1 restated: _____

_____

Support idea 1: _____

_____

Support idea 2: _____

_____

Support idea 3: _____

_____

Paragraph 3: Reason 2 supported

Reason 2 restated: _____

_____

Support idea 1: _____

_____

Support idea 2: _____

_____

Support idea 3: _____

_____

Paragraph 4: Reason 3 supported

Reason 3 restated: _____

_____

Support idea 1: _____

_____

Support idea 2: _____

_____

Support idea 3: _____

_____

Paragraph 5: Summary

Restate position with most important point. _____

_____

_____

Make a statement or two regarding the importance of your position. _____

_____

_____

_____

Writing Templates

Name

Prewriting Activity: Brainstorming

Write as much information as you can about both sides of the issue.

Position 1 is: _____

_____

_____

_____

Position 2 is: _____

_____

_____

_____

Position 1	Position 2

Name

Considering Alternatives and Compromises

Before taking a position on a issue it is important to consider compromises and alternatives. This does not mean that you must choose to support a compromise or alternative, but understanding them and being aware of them will help you better support your own position.

Four Possible Alternatives Are:

1. _____

_____

_____

_____

2. _____

_____

_____

_____

3. _____

_____

_____

_____

4. _____

_____

_____

_____

Four Possible Compromises Are:

1. _____

_____

_____

_____

_____

2. _____

_____

_____

_____

_____

3. _____

_____

_____

_____

_____

4. _____

_____

_____

_____

_____

Name _____

What I Think

I think _____

Three reasons I think this are _____

_____

• One reason I think this is _____

_____

I know this because _____

_____

• The second reason I think this is _____

This is true because _____

• The last reason I think this is _____

_____

I know this because _____

_____

I think _____

because _____

_____

_____

_____

_____

_____

_____

_____

What I Think

Paragraph 1: Introduction and three reasons that support my position

My position is _____

_____

Reason 1: _____

_____

Reason 2: _____

_____

Reason 3: _____

_____

Paragraph 2: Reason 1 supported

Reason 1 restated: _____

_____

Support idea 1: _____

_____

Support idea 2: _____

_____

Support idea 3: _____

_____

Paragraph 3: Reason 2 supported

Reason 2 restated: _____

_____

Support idea 1: _____

_____

Support idea 2: _____

_____

Support idea 3: _____

_____

Paragraph 4: Reason 3 supported

Reason 3 restated: _____

_____

Support idea 1: _____

_____

Support idea 2: _____

_____

Support idea 3: _____

_____

Paragraph 5: Summary to include a restatement of my position and the most important point. It should state a reason why my position is important.

Summary: _____

_____

_____

Make a statement or two regarding the importance of your position. _____

_____

_____

_____

Name _____

What I Think

Paragraph 1: Make an attention-getting comment. It can be a quote, fact, anecdote . . .

_____

_____

_____

_____

_____

_____

Paragraph 2: Position and an introduction to your argument. Each reason that you use to support your position should be introduced here.

Position Statement

_____

Reason Statements (3 to 5)

_____

_____

_____

_____

_____

_____

Paragraph 3: Reason 1 restated and supported

_____

_____

_____

_____

_____

_____

Paragraph 4 : Reason 2 restated and supported

_____

_____

_____

_____

_____

_____

_____

Paragraph 5: Reason 3 restated and supported

_____

_____

_____

_____

_____

_____

_____

Closing Paragraph: Summary of argument to include most important points, possibly an anecdote or story, and a statement of importance of your position.

_____

_____

_____

_____

_____

_____

_____

_____

_____